Children and Young People as Action Researchers

WITHDRAWN

Children and Young People as Action Researchers:

A practical guide to supporting pupil voice in schools

RITA CHEMINAIS

Open University Press

Open University Press
McGraw-Hill Education
McGraw-Hill House
Shoppenhangers Road
Maidenhead
Berkshire
England
SL6 2QL

email: enquiries@openup.co.uk
world wide web: www.openup.co.uk

and

Two Penn Plaza, New York, NY 10121-2289, USA

First published 2012
Copyright © Rita Cheminais, 2012

A catalogue record of this book is available from the British Library

ISBN-13: 9780335246465 (pb)
ISBN-10: 033524646X (pb)
e-ISBN: 9780335246472

Library of Congress Cataloging-in-Publication Data
CIP data has been applied for

Typeset by Graphicraft
Printed in the UK by Bell and Bain Ltd, Glasgow.

Fictitious names of companies, products, people, characters and/or data that may be used
herein (in case studies or in examples) are not intended to represent any real individual,
company, product or event.

MIX
Paper from
responsible sources
FSC® C007785
FSC
www.fsc.org

The McGraw·Hill Companies

Contents

List of figures

List of tables

Acknowledgements

This handbook, with accompanying phase-specific resource packs for pupils, is dedicated to all those wonderful children and young people I have met in primary and secondary schools across the UK, who have shared with me the amazing pupil-led research activities they have been doing, which have made a huge difference to the learning, achievements and well-being of their peers.

I wish to thank all the visionary, dynamic and innovative school leaders and senior managers I have worked with in the same schools, who have truly empowered their pupils to take an active role in school decision-making, in order to bring about change and improvement for the benefit of other pupils.

In particular, I wish to acknowledge the stunning and outstanding practice in pupil 'voice' and pupil-led action research at the following schools: Goose Green Primary and Nursery School in East Dulwich; Hillyfield Academy, Walthamstow in Waltham Forest; Tadley Community Primary School in Hampshire; Alder Community High School in Tameside; Aldridge School – a Science College in Walsall, West Midlands; and Calderstones School – a Specialist Science College in Liverpool. Their outstanding practice features as cameos in Chapter 2.

I would like to thank Dave Harrison and Beryl Oliver, Associate Education Consultants with Educational Consultancy & Management (ECM) Solutions, for working with some of my award schools, in order to enable me to write this book.

I would also like to thank Dr Monika Lee, my commissioning editor at Open University Press, for supporting the original book proposal and for giving me insightful feedback during the writing of this practical guide. My thanks also go to Laura Givans, Editorial Assistant with Open University Press and McGraw-Hill Education, for providing guidance on submitting the manuscript for this book.

Finally, I wish to thank Philip Eastwood, Advanced Skills Teacher for Initial Teacher Training at St Mary and St Paul's Church of England Primary School in Prescot, Merseyside, for continuing to encourage and inspire me to write practical books that make a real difference to teachers and pupils work across the UK and abroad.

Abbreviations

CD	compact disc
DVD	digital versatile disc
ECM	Educational Consultancy & Management
ENDA	Environmental Development Action in the Third World
ESRC	Economic and Social Research Council
FE	further education
ICSEI	International Congress for School Effectiveness and Improvement
ICT	information and communications technology
KS	key stage
PDA	personal digital assistant
PRU	pupil referral unit
TV	television
UK	United Kingdom
UNCRC	United Nations Convention on the Rights of the Child
USB	universal serial bus
VAK	visual, auditory, kinaesthetic
VLE	virtual learning environment

Introduction

This handbook, with accompanying phase-specific resource materials on CD-ROM for pupils, has been written specifically for those senior leaders and teachers in primary and secondary schools, and in post-16 provision, who are partners in pupil-led action research. The intention of the resources is to act as a springboard and essential step-by-step guide for pupils as researchers and for the senior manager or teacher who is overseeing the pupil-led action research project within the educational setting.

The total package of resources enables pupils as researchers, and senior managers or teachers guiding pupils through the action research process, to:

- understand the concept, principles and process of pupil-led action research;
- know which are the most appropriate research approaches to use;
- develop the essential knowledge, skills and personal qualities of an action researcher;
- know what to include in a final written research report;
- know the best ways to present research findings to different audiences;
- explore the potential to gain external validation for their good practice in pupil-led action research.

Each chapter in this handbook provides an overview of the main topics to be covered in the action research journey. Each offers practical tips and guidance; useful resources that can be downloaded or photocopied for use by pupils; cameos of good practice in pupil-led action research; and further activities for pupils to explore and think about.

In addition, a number of resources are included on the accompanying CD-ROM:

- **Primary phase pupil action research resource pack.** This pack is designed for use by the team of nominated primary-aged action researchers, supported by a member of staff, overseeing the Change for Children Award process in the educational setting. The pack is written in age-appropriate language, but can be customised and tailored to suit the school or academy context. The resource pack covers the following topics: what to research in a school; how to work as a research team; choosing and using different research tools; how to make sense of research evidence; how to present research findings; sharing the good practice with others.
- **Secondary phase pupil action research pack.** This pack is designed for use by the team of nominated action researchers of secondary school or further education (FE) college age. The member of staff overseeing the Change for Children award process will be able to guide the pupils or students in working their way through the action research resource pack. The pack is written in age-appropriate language for young people aged from 11 to 19. The pack covers the following topics: what to investigate in school or college; working collaboratively as a team of young action researchers; choosing and piloting

different research methods; undertaking the action research fieldwork; analysing and interpreting research data; presenting the research findings; sharing the action research good practice with other schools, academies, pupil referral units (PRUs) and FE colleges.

- **PowerPoint presentation on the Change for Children Award process.** This PowerPoint presentation can be used by an external consultant from Educational Consultancy & Management (ECM) Solutions or by the senior member of staff overseeing the pupil/ student-led action research project in the educational setting. It offers an introduction and overview of the entire award process for governors and staff. The presentation covers the following: the stages in the award journey; the benefits of engaging in the award process; the resources used by the pupils/students to self-review and further develop their skills as action researchers; the type of evidence to gather to build the electronic portfolio; and an example of a typical on-site one-day final assessment.

- **PowerPoint presentation introducing pupils/students to action research.** This PowerPoint presentation is designed to be delivered by the external consultant from Educational Consultancy & Management (ECM) Solutions, or by the senior member of staff overseeing the pupil/student-led action research project. It provides the children and young people with an overview of and an introduction to what action research entails. The presentation defines what action research is; the skills action researchers needs to develop; the steps in an action research project; examples of the most popular research methods; examples of the different type of research data to collect; different ways of presenting research data; how to keep a research diary; and what to include in a final research report. The presentation can be tailored to suit different contexts and ages of children and young people.

The inspiration and idea for this resource arose as a result of all the wonderful pupil-led action research projects and activities I have had the privilege to discover on my travels to the many good and outstanding schools, academies, PRUs, FE and sixth-form colleges throughout the UK, in my role as a freelance education consultant.

It is hoped that the resource will inspire and encourage many other educational settings to engage their pupils in powerful action research. As schools, academies, PRUs and colleges are encouraged by the government to work more closely together in clusters or federations, the opportunity to undertake joint pupil-led action research across a family of schools, in addition to sharing their good practice in this aspect of their work, becomes ever more crucial in the current educational climate. Empowering pupils and giving them a greater voice and choice and opportunity to contribute to whole-school decision-making strengthens their rights and responsibilities under the United Nations Convention on the Rights of the Child (UNCRC) in relation to Articles 12 ('The child's right to express and have his or her views given due weight in all matters affecting them') and 13 ('The child's right to freedom of expression – to seek, receive and impart information orally, in writing or in print, in art form or through any other media of the child's choice').

Teachers and pupils alike, as co-learners and partners in the school improvement process, each bring their own perspective on how to ensure children and young people achieve more, have a high standard of well-being and enjoy a positive educational experience that will prepare them for life after school and college. Listening to the views of pupils, and understanding the findings from pupil-led action research on matters relating to teaching, learning, the curriculum, school policy, environment and organisation are important in ensuring that the right decisions are made by school leaders, in order to meet the needs of learners in the twenty-first century.

Genuine participation of pupils in a school can only happen when they are truly empowered by teachers, to take the lead in exploring some of the issues which directly affect their lives. Teachers need to feel confident to 'let go' and give greater ownership to pupils over their learning and well-being. Similarly, pupils need to feel empowered, responsible and able to take risks in their learning. Pupil-led action research enables this to happen by allowing children and young people to become agents of change, thereby putting them at the heart of influencing school decision-making.

It is important to remember that children have the expert knowledge of what it is like to be a child, not adults. Children and young people see things from a very different perspective than adults. They have different and more immediate concerns about issues in school that affect their lives than teachers do. If you really want to make a difference to the lives and outcomes of pupils or students learning in a range of educational settings, then this resource is for you, whether you are a pupil, student, teacher, senior manager, head teacher or principal. Enjoy the learning journey and using this practical resource.

Note on the use of the term 'pupils'

The term 'pupils' is used throughout the book, and refers equally to 'students', 'children' and 'young people' educated in schools, academies, PRUs, FE and sixth-form colleges.

Pupils as action researchers: the basics

The topics covered in this chapter include:

- What is action research?
- The benefits of pupils doing action research
- Choosing what to research
- The ethics and principles of action research
- The action research cycle
- The role of the teacher overseeing the pupil-led action research
- Forming a pupil-led action research team
- The skills and qualities required to become an action researcher
- Coaching and mentoring pupils as action researchers
- Further activities for pupils as action researchers to think about

This chapter is to be used in conjunction with Sections 1, 2 and 3 of the relevant phase-specific pupil research resource pack, by the teacher overseeing pupil-led action research in the educational setting.

What is action research?

Action research entails finding out, establishing the truth and gaining a better understanding about a concern, issue or problem raised by a group of pupils, usually through the school council. It involves investigating or exploring the issue further by undertaking research, to gather evidence in the form of information (data), which is analysed and interpreted to reach a conclusion and make recommendations, to inform decision-making, in order to bring about the right change or improvement for the benefit of the pupils concerned.

Pupils can effect change in their own school or college by making sure that the teachers who make the decisions know exactly what pupils think and what they want, as a result of pupil-led action research. If pupils do not get involved in the decision-making process, then they are likely to get only what the teachers and other adults in the school think they want.

The benefits of pupils doing action research

There are many benefits to pupils doing action research in their own school or college:

- gaining a greater sense of pride and satisfaction in solving a problem, and making a change or improvement in school that benefits other peers;
- developing useful life skills;
- developing good communication skills in being able to relate to children and adults in different ways;
- learning how to work cooperatively with other pupils from different cultures, gender and age groups in a pupil-led action research team;
- learning how to become a reflective critical thinker;
- learning how to work with teachers as partners and co-learners in an action research project;
- gaining greater self-confidence and feeling good about themselves;
- understanding how decisions are made and change happens in school;
- improving the use and application of multi-media and information and communications technology (ICT) when researching a pupil issue and analysing and presenting data;
- feeling respected, listened to and taken seriously by teachers and other adults in the school or college.

Choosing what to research

The top tips listed in Figure 1.1 offer staff overseeing pupil-led action research, guidance on how best to support and advise pupil researchers in deciding what to research, when a number of pupil topics or issues have been raised.

1. Encourage pupils to choose the issue or problem to research that is of most concern to the majority of pupils in the educational setting.
2. Ensure research on the issue selected is manageable in the given time.
3. Find out if any previous research has been done on the topic or issue in the school, or in other schools, in order to guide the work of the pupil research team.
4. Be very clear about exactly what the pupil-led research team wants to find out about the issue or concern.
5. Turn the pupil issue or concern into a key question and consider forming a **hypothesis**, i.e. a possible answer or explanation to the question raised.
6. Advise pupil researchers to select suitable research methods that will not cause any major disruption to the work of other pupils or teachers in the educational setting.
7. Ensure the pupil research team shares their initial thoughts about the pupil concern or issue raised, with the head teacher, to sound them out.
8. Ensure the permission of the head teacher has been obtained before the pupils start to do any action research in the educational setting.

Figure 1.1 Top tips on guiding pupils in choosing what to research

Popular topics for pupil-led action research

Pupil-led research tends to focus on the aspects of the life and work of a school, as illustrated in Table 1.1. However, pupil researchers may have other topics or issues raised by pupils which are not included on the list. If so, that is OK, and it may be helpful to identify which area they fit in with.

Table 1.1 Popular topics chosen for pupil-led action research

Teaching and learning	School policy and curriculum
• What are the features of good teaching? • What makes a good lesson? • What makes a good lesson starter? • What makes a good lesson ending? • What helps pupils to learn best? • What are the most popular preferred learning styles of pupils? • What makes learning fun and enjoyable? • What helps pupils to remember what they have learned? • What is the best classroom environment for learning? • What helps pupils to become more independent learners?	• What would make the curriculum more interesting and relevant to pupils? • How can ICT and multi-media be used more effectively to improve curriculum delivery? • What more can be done to help pupils make the right curriculum choices? • How can the curriculum be made more inclusive to reflect cultural differences? • What other after-school activities would pupils welcome? • How can pupils become more involved in assessing and reviewing their own progress? • How can homework be made more interesting and meaningful for pupils? • How can the school's behaviour policy be made more pupil-friendly?
The school's organisation and environment	**Pupil well-being**
• What more can be done to improve outdoor play facilities for pupils? • What can be done to provide quiet areas for pupils in school and in the school grounds? • What common room facilities could be provided for pupils in school when the weather is bad? • How can the school grounds be made more pleasant? • What can be done to improve the pupil toilets? • What changes could be made to the school timetable and/or to the school day to enhance pupils' social and learning opportunities?	• What could be done to make transfer to the next school or college better for pupils? • What makes a good form tutor? • What makes a good head of year? • How can pupils be helped in school if they have worries or concerns? • How can the school dining experience for pupils be improved? • How can the safety of pupils be further improved at break and at lunchtimes? • How can pupils become more involved in community projects? • How can pupils gain a better understanding about local business and enterprise?

The ethics of action research

The **ethics** or **code of conduct** of research refers to making sure that the well-being, interests and concerns of those taking part in the research are looked after and respected. The research must not cause harm to or upset any participants at any time.

The principles of undertaking action research

The following principles will help pupils as action researchers to undertake ethical research:

• Always ensure the pupil researchers introduce themselves to the pupils or adults participating in the research.
• Anyone who is going to be asked to take part in the research must be told: what the purpose of the research is; the methods of research being used; what their participation will involve; how the information will be recorded and used; and how the outcome of the research will be publicised.

- Ensure pupil researchers give those agreeing to take part in the research reassurance about confidentiality and anonymity in the information and responses they provide.
- When interviewing, ask one question at a time.
- Avoid asking leading questions.
- Give pupils and adults time to answer the question asked.
- Keep the language used in questions simple and straightforward.
- Ensure pupil researchers have been given written approval to undertake the research from the head teacher, and have also obtained parental consent.
- Keep pupils, teachers, governors and the head teacher up to date with the progress of the action research.
- Allow those involved in the research to check the accuracy of their responses.
- Always obtain permission from those involved in the research to use any of their quotations or video extracts in the final research report, and in any research presentation, but ensure they remain anonymous.
- Report research findings in the best way to suit the different audiences.
- Do not force pupils or teachers to take part in the research if they do not wish to do so.
- Avoid influencing the responses or opinions of those participating in the research.
- Ensure pupil researchers remain open-minded and unbiased when undertaking the research.
- Make it clear to those taking part in the research that they have the right to withdraw from the research at any stage, if they do not wish to continue.
- Ensure pupil researchers always thank those taking part in the research and explain what will happen next.

The action research cycle

The simplest way to conduct action research involves the plan–act–evaluate–reflect cycle. Figure 1.2 illustrates the main stages in the action research process that pupil researchers will need to go through in order to meet the requirements expected, particularly if the school wishes to achieve the UK Change for Children Award, available from Educational Consultancy & Management (ECM) Solutions.

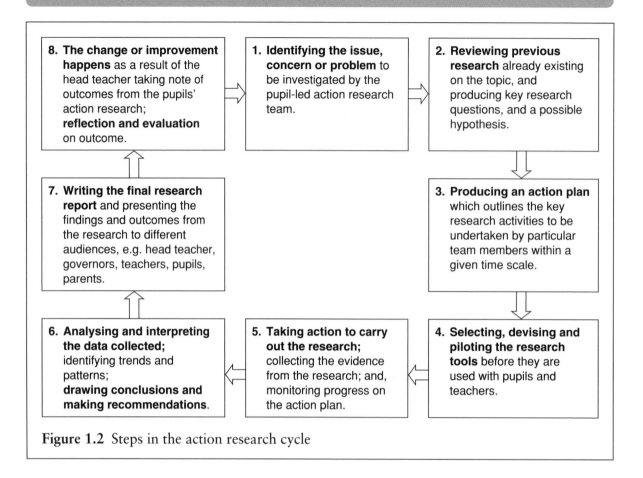

Figure 1.2 Steps in the action research cycle

Steps in planning and doing the research

Pupils as researchers will need to consider the following steps when planning and undertaking the action research in school:

1. What is the major issue, problem or question to be researched?
2. Define the issue, problem or question in clear, pupil-friendly language.
3. What is known already about the topic? Has anyone else in the educational setting explored the issue before?
4. What is the key purpose of doing the research? Will the research help to improve decision-making in the educational setting?
5. What is the hypothesis? (What do pupil researchers think the answer will be?)
6. Select, prepare and try out the appropriate research tools to answer the question, solve the problem or resolve the issue or concern.
7. Undertake the research to collect the required information (data).
8. Analyse and interpret the data and present it in a user-friendly way.
9. Produce a research report which makes fair and accurate conclusions and recommendations, based on secure research evidence.
10. Evaluate and reflect upon the research. Did pupils as researchers get the information they wanted, in order to make the change or improvement happen?

The role of the teacher overseeing the pupil-led action research

The deputy head teacher or assistant head teacher or teacher overseeing the pupil-led action research project will act as a facilitator to support the smooth running of the research. They will step back to allow pupils to get on with the action research in school, and will not lead the process. Other key roles the senior member of staff or teacher will play are as follows:

- Encourage, prompt and give approval to pupils to do the research.
- Act as a 'critical friend' to pupil researchers, offering impartial advice and guidance when required.
- Train and prepare pupils in using different research tools and methods.
- Help with the printing of research surveys and questionnaires.
- Act as a go-between with staff and pupils participating in the research.
- Alert pupil action researchers to any potential problems or difficulties that may arise when doing the research.
- Help to resolve any tensions that may arise in the pupil-led research team.
- Act as an advocate and champion for pupil-led action research in school.
- Respect pupils as researchers in their own right.
- Provide coaching and mentoring to pupils undertaking action research.
- Be approachable and available to pupil researchers, attending the pupil-led action research team meetings.
- Help pupil researchers to analyse, interpret and present quantitative and qualitative data, in order to identify any patterns, trends or similarities.
- Be willing to learn from pupils as action researchers.
- Negotiate administrative support for the pupil-led action research team, as and when required.
- Encourage less confident pupils to take on research roles, with the support of more experienced pupil researchers.

Forming a pupil-led action research team

When forming a pupil-led action research team, there are some key factors that need to be considered:

- How will pupils be selected to be members of the research team?
- Will the pupil-led research team be inclusive, e.g. have pupils of different age ranges, abilities, gender and cultural backgrounds on it?
- How many pupils will be on the pupil-led action research team? (The ideal number of pupils on a research team is between six and eight.
- Which pupil is best placed to be the leader of the research team?
- Who will train, coach and mentor pupils in action research methods?
- How and when will the action research training be delivered to the pupil researchers?
- What roles will the various pupils on the action research team undertake?
- Where, and how often, will the pupil-led action research team meet?
- Who will plan and organise the agendas for the pupil-led action research team meetings?
- How much budget will the pupil-led action team require, and who will manage and oversee this?
- What will be the agreed pupil-led action research team ground rules?
- Who will replace a pupil researcher if they leave the team?

Recruiting pupils to join the pupil-led action research team

The deputy head teacher, assistant head teacher or teacher responsible for overseeing pupil voice and pupils as action researchers is likely to consult the school council regarding the recruitment of pupil researchers to form the pupil-led action research team in the educational setting.

- An advertisement will need to be developed in consultation with pupils on the school council, to invite pupils in the school to apply to be action researchers.
- The recruitment and application process will need to be agreed, i.e. whether it will be by pupil nomination in form groups, or by written application, podcast or blog from any interested pupils in the educational setting.
- When and who will be involved in the shortlisting process?
- What will the format of the selection process entail, e.g. an interview, a presentation or both?
- Who will be on the interview panel and how many will be pupils?
- What will be the title of the presentation for shortlisted pupils?
- How many interview questions will be set and what will these cover?
- When and where will the interviews take place in school?

Figures 1.3a and 1.3b provide a model advertisement for recruiting pupil action researchers in the secondary and primary phase of education, respectively. Figure 1.4 provides a model job description for a pupil researcher. Figure 1.5 provides an example of possible interview questions to ask prospective pupil researchers.

HAVE YOU GOT WHAT IT TAKES TO BE AN ACTION RESEARCHER?

EIGHT pupils from across the school are required to investigate and explore an issue raised by the School Council, which needs to be made better for other pupils.

INTERESTED?

If you would like to become one of the eight action researchers, then go to Reception in school and request an application pack.

Completed applications must be given to the deputy head teacher by midday on 2 February.

Interviews for shortlisted pupils will be held on 16 February.

Figure 1.3a Advertisement for recruiting pupil researchers in secondary schools

HAVE YOU GOT WHAT IT TAKES TO BE AN ACTION RESEARCHER?

EIGHT pupils from across the school are required to research an issue raised by the School Council, which needs to be made better for other pupils.

INTERESTED?

If you would like to become one of the eight action researchers, then go to Reception in school and ask for an application pack.

Completed applications must be given to the deputy head teacher by 12.00 on 2 February.

Interviews for shortlisted pupils will be held on 16 February.

Figure 1.3b Advertisement for recruiting pupil researchers in primary schools

JOB TITLE: Pupil action researcher

RESPONSIBLE TO: The Chair of the School Council, and the deputy head teacher overseeing pupil research

MAIN DUTIES

1. To undertake research in school, under the direction of the Chair of the School Council, and the leader of the pupil action research team.
2. To engage in initial training in research methods.
3. To attend all the meetings of the pupil action research team and to report on progress and findings from research.
4. To work cooperatively with other members of the pupil action research team.
5. To seek guidance, as and when required, from the deputy head teacher and from the leader of the pupil action research team.
6. To analyse and interpret research information (data).
7. To present findings from research in different formats for a range of audiences.
8. To contribute information to the final written research report.
9. To participate in contributing evidence to the Change for Children Award.
10. To undertake any other relevant action research duties, as required by the team leader and/or the Chair of the School Council.

Figure 1.4 Example of a job description for a pupil action researcher

1. Why do you want to be a member of the pupil-led action research team?
2. What skills would you bring to the pupil action research team?
3. How will you cope with working within a set timescale or deadline?
4. Can you give us a recent example of when you have explored or researched something in school?
5. How would you present your research findings to the head teacher and the governing body?
6. How would you present your research findings to the School Council?
7. How would you ensure confidentiality in the responses given by pupils and teachers during research?
8. Are there any questions you wish to ask the interview panel about the action research post?
9. Are you still a firm candidate for the post of pupil action researcher?

Figure 1.5 Examples of questions for pupil action researcher interview

The skills and qualities required to become an action researcher

Table 1.2 shows the skills and qualities essential to pupils who wish to become action researchers.

Table 1.2 Essential skills and qualities of pupil researchers

Skills	Qualities
• Confident at interviewing adults and pupils, asking open questions • Good note taker • Able to identify important actions from observations • Confident in using multi-media technology to capture first-hand evidence • Able to apply and use ICT for research • Able to make judgements based on secure evidence • Able to collect, analyse and interpret research data • Able to summarise key research findings, draw conclusions and make recommendations • Able to produce a written research report • Able to remain impartial and unbiased when doing research • Able to deliver presentations on research findings to a range of different audiences • Able to think quickly and work under pressure within a set timescale	• A good listener • Patient • Trustworthy • Good time-keeper • Reliable • Understanding and sympathetic • Tactful • Diplomatic • Fair • Open and honest • Self-confident • Good communicator • Well organised • Use initiative • Cooperative

Within any pupil-led action research team, particular members will bring certain talents, skills and knowledge to the overall work of the team. For example, some pupil researchers will be able to:

- put their ideas into practice;
- make best use of resources;
- inspire other team members;
- create a good team spirit;
- ask the right questions;
- be analytical and a critical thinker;
- solve problems;
- weigh up and judge different options;
- respond sensitively to the feelings of others;
- finish tasks on time;
- organise their own research work and that of others successfully;
- bring specialist knowledge of and skills in a research method or a topic.

Figure 1.6 provides a useful checklist for the pupil-led action research team leader to use, in order to review the overall team skills.

- All team members are clear about their role
- Pupil researchers understand how their role fits in with the work of the team as a whole
- There is a good level of mutual trust and respect existing in the team
- All members of the pupil-led action research team have an understanding of basic research methods
- All team members understand the basics of decision-making and enabling change to happen
- All team members have access to coaching and/or mentoring in relation to developing their ongoing research skills
- Action research team meetings take place regularly
- All team members have an opportunity to share ideas, information and good practice
- All team members' views are listened to and respected
- All team members feel valued for the contributions they make
- Tasks are distributed equally across the members of the team

Figure 1.6 Checklist for the teacher overseeing the pupil research team

Coaching and mentoring pupils as action researchers

Following an initial team session to introduce pupil researchers to the range of different action research methods available, it is important that the senior member of staff or teacher overseeing the work of the pupil-led action research team provides regular coaching or mentoring sessions with individual or a small group of pupil researchers from the action research team.

What is the difference between coaching and mentoring? **Coaching**, in relation to action research, is an ongoing process that helps to develop a particular aspect of a pupil's practice in doing research in school. It does not tell the pupil what to do but helps them to find their own best way of doing the research. **Mentoring**, in the context of action research, is the process of supporting pupils as learners in research, to manage to cope with any significant change or problems that may arise during the research project.

Older pupils, experienced in action research, may also provide coaching or mentoring to other pupils who are new to the role of undertaking school-based research. Figure 1.7 provides a useful framework for use in a pupil researcher coaching or mentoring session. This can be tailored to suit the context of the school.

Coach or mentor: _____

Pupil researcher: _____

Date of coaching or mentoring session: _____

Focus of the coaching or mentoring session:

Points arising from discussion	Coach/mentor comments, questions and feedback

Figure 1.7 Framework for a pupil researcher coaching or mentoring session

Further activities to do with pupils as action researchers relating to Sections 1, 2 and 3 in the relevant pupil research resource pack

Pupil action researchers will find it useful to discuss the following questions with the senior member of staff overseeing and guiding their research project:

1. What do you want to find out or discover by doing the research?
2. How will your action research lead you to a better understanding about the issue or problem raised by other pupils in the school?
3. What practical resources do you need as a pupil-led action research team in order to undertake the research?
4. What will be your plan of action for doing the research in school, within the agreed timescale?

CHAPTER

2 Choosing the right research methods

The topics covered in this chapter include:

- What should be covered in a research skills training course for pupils
- Which research methods should be chosen
- Popular research methods
- Advantages and disadvantages of each research method
- Top tips for using each research method
- Examples of research tools
- Cameos of good practice in pupil-led action research
- Keeping a reflective research journal, diary or log
- Sampling
- Further activities for pupils as action researchers to think about

This chapter is to be used in conjunction with Sections 4 and 5 of the relevant phase-specific pupil research pack, by the teacher overseeing pupil-led action research in the educational setting.

What should be covered in a research skills training course for pupils?

The greatest barrier pupils face in relation to becoming effective action researchers is a lack of knowledge about research skills, due to them not having received any training in such skills, either from within or beyond the school, prior to doing an action research project.

The content of a training session or course on research skills for pupils should cover the following aspects:

- **Introduction to research** – what it is; why it is important; the types of research; the different research tools, skills and approaches
- **Other people's research** – what can be learned from this; how to access, critique and summarise the research of others on the same topic or issue
- **The relationship between research and the truth** – fact or opinion; bias
- **The ethics of doing research** – participants' rights; ethical dilemmas; confidentiality and anonymity
- **Getting started on a research project** – how to identify an area or topic to research; how to form the research questions and a hypothesis

- **Data handling** – how to collect, analyse, interpret and present qualitative and quantitative information (data)
- **Presenting the research findings** – what to include in a final research report; how to present research findings to a range of different audiences

The training can be delivered over a number of weeks, well in advance of the start of the pupil-led action research project. Each training session should include a practical element, where pupils can practise skills and use different research tools. The training can be delivered to an individual school or college, or it may be more cost-effective to deliver research skills training to a cluster of schools' pupil researchers.

Which research methods should be chosen?

When choosing which research methods to use it is important to select the right ones, otherwise the wrong method will affect the quality of the results and the accuracy of the findings. No one method of collecting information (data) is better than another. The research methods to choose depend on four factors:

- the nature of the topic or issue being researched;
- the nature of the participants being engaged in the research;
- the type of information (data) needing to be gathered, e.g. qualitative, quantitative or both;
- the timescale in which the research is to be undertaken.

It is good practice to use a variety of research methods in order to cross-check (triangulate) the evidence gathered from different people, e.g. whether pupils, teachers and other key stakeholders have similar or different views on the issue being researched.

The teacher overseeing the work of the pupil action research team will be able to advise, but not dictate, which research methods will be the best to use within the school context.

Popular research methods

Before looking in more detail at the most common and popular research methods used by pupils in schools, it is helpful to note the difference between two sources of information (data) that are likely to be collected, from using a range of research methods.

Primary sources are information (data) that pupils as researchers will collect themselves directly from the participants engaging with the research.

Secondary sources are information (data) that is already available, which has already been gathered by others. For example:

- official government statistics, reports and papers;
- information from the mass media – TV, radio, newspapers, magazines, advertisements, films, videos, blogs, podcasts;
- books and journals;
- information from national and voluntary organisations, e.g. the Children's Society, the National Children's Bureau;
- information from other schools and colleges research on the same topic.

When using secondary sources of information (data) it will need to be decided:

- how reliable the information is;
- whether the information is free from bias (check this by doing a content analysis);
- whether the information adds something new to the research.

Content analysis

This is an important approach used by researchers to check out secondary sources of information for any bias or distortion of the facts, particularly in articles that may appear in newspapers, on TV or in radio programmes.

When undertaking content analysis of any secondary sources of information pupil researchers will need to count, highlight or list the number of words in the article or programme that give a negative, misleading or favourable perspective on the subject or topic.

Pupil researchers will also need to highlight any factual information in the secondary information source, and check it out to ensure it is accurate. In addition, pupil researchers will need to check if the various forms of media treat the same topic in different ways. This not only relates to the printed word, but also to any visual images, for example as used in advertisements.

Statistical information produced by the government on the topic being explored needs to enable pupil researchers to make comparisons with their own small-scale research findings.

Methods of research to gather primary sources of information

The most common methods used to collect primary sources of information (data) from participants include the following:

- questionnaire or survey;
- interview – structured and semi-structured;
- observation;
- experiment.

Table 2.1 provides a useful at-a-glance guide to the different research methods listed above, outlining their advantages and disadvantages, and in which contexts they are most appropriate to use.

Table 2.1 Popular research methods to collect primary sources of information (data)

Research method	Questionnaire and Survey	Interview	Observation	Experiment
Definition	**Questionnaire** is a written form of a structured interview, which uses largely closed questions to gather statistical descriptive quantitative data on an issue or topic. **Survey** is used to gain a general picture of people's views, opinions and attitudes and uses more open questions.	**Interview** is used to identify people's views, preferences, attitudes and beliefs about a particular issue or topic. **Structured interview** uses largely closed questions, which limit free response. **Semi-structured interview** uses a core set of key questions with follow-up questions to gain further insight.	**Observation** is about listening and watching carefully what is taking place in a particular context. The researcher may use a structured observation schedule with predetermined criteria, which can be coded or tallied, or a blank piece of paper to record actions. **Direct observation** entails observing without joining in with those being watched. **Participant observation** is where the researcher observes what is going on while engaging with the group action.	**Experiment** is used to discover the effect of variables on participants' behaviour, outcomes or results. It is concerned with cause and effect. Variables may include age, gender, culture, group size.
Advantages	Used with a large number of people Good response rate where it is anonymous Useful for gathering factual statistical data Uses closed questions which reduces bias Enables comparisons to be made	Gives high-quality data Collects people's opinions, thinking and motivation Offers greater insight into people's views on a topic Can use closed and open questions Offers the interviewer greater flexibility to adjust questions or probe interviewee further	People are observed in natural settings Provides a deeper and richer understanding Useful to observe people over a period of time Offers qualitative and quantitative data	Helps to identify people's reactions Useful for making comparisons Helps to inform problem-solving
Disadvantages	Information is largely descriptive Participants may not interpret questions correctly Provides limited in-depth information (questionnaire)	Time-consuming process to undertake interviews and transcribe findings Can only be used with a small number of participants Participants may give the responses they think you want to hear	Observer may influence the behaviour of those being observed Observer may miss some events during observation due to filling in an observation schedule Time-consuming process	Time-consuming process Requires consistent conditions, which may be more problematic to set up

Tips on use	Be clear about the data you want to get from participants. Draft out questions and pilot survey or questionnaire. Provide simple instructions in introduction – why researching this topic; where to return the completed questionnaire or survey; and timescale for completion. Avoid using technical jargon. Give a guarantee of confidentiality and anonymity. Promise feedback on findings.	Decide how many people to interview. Seek permission to interview, particularly if you wish to video- or audio-record the interview. Plan interviews – time per interview, how many questions, open and closed. Pilot the interviews first. Interview in a suitable quiet area. Undertake paired interviews – a partner to write responses and you to ask questions. Introduce yourself to the interviewee and explain why you are doing the research. Make good eye contact and be an active listener. Ask easy questions first and then more open questions. Enable interviewee to ask you any questions. Check you have understood the interviewee's responses by repeating back what they said and asking 'Is that what you meant?' Thank the interviewee for taking part in the interview.	Be clear about the focus of the observation. Get permission to observe. Decide whether you will use an observation schedule or video-record the observation. Decide on the type of observation – direct or participant observation. Draw up a timetable for when the observations will take place. Be clear about how you will record the findings from an observation, e.g. notes, tally or coding system. Make a note of any problems met when doing the observations, and how you might improve the process if you did it again.	Obtain permission to undertake the experiment. Check that the experiment is useful to do and enhances other research methods. Plan and prepare in advance for what the experiment will entail. Ensure the experiment occurs under the same consistent conditions. Make clear notes on the results of the experiment, i.e. what the experiment revealed. Indicate how the experiment could be improved if it was done again.
When to use	Where you need to gather information from a large representative sample	When you need to gain a smaller focused view on a topic or issue from individuals or from a small group	Where you need to observe participants in a particular context, e.g. classroom, school canteen, or in a particular subject area	Within a particular lesson or classroom context

Examples of research tools

Figures 4.1 to 4.6 in the relevant phase-specific pupil research resource pack offer examples of the types of research tools pupil researchers may wish to develop for their own school-based small-scale action research project.

These can be further customised to suit the context of the education setting and the age of the participating pupils.

Cameos of good practice in pupil-led action research

The following six cameos of good practice in pupil-led action research in maintained mainstream primary and secondary schools across the UK can be shared with pupil researchers before they undertake their own school-based research, to enable them to have a clearer idea of how research works in practice.

Cameo of good practice – ECO Warriors environmental audit

School: Goose Green Primary & Nursery School, East Dulwich, Southwark

Focus of the pupil research: Identifying the school's strengths and areas for further improvement in relation to saving energy, recycling, protecting wildlife and the environment.

Who was involved: A small group of pupils from the ECO Warriors team within the school.

What the pupil researchers did: The ECO Warriors undertook an environmental audit around the school, including the school grounds. The ECO Warriors met together following the audit to discuss the findings, and draw up an action plan to carry out a range of environmental activities to address any gaps arising from the audit.

Outcomes from the research:

- The ECO Team recruited two representatives from each year group in the school.
- The school achieved the ECO Schools Bronze Award for being a sustainable school.
- The ECO Warrior team undertook 'The Big Tidy Up' which entailed pupils litter picking in the school grounds and in the local area surrounding the school.
- A 'Bug Hotel' was created in the school grounds.
- A 'Fence Project' was started in order to plant a living shield along the school perimeter fence.
- School rules were drawn up to promote economical printing and photocopying.
- Unwanted towels were collected to donate to the RSPCA East Winch Wildlife Centre in Norfolk to keep sick seal pups warm.

Cameo of good practice – The pupil Learning Council research pupils' learning

School: Hillyfield Academy, Walthamstow, Waltham Forest

Focus of the pupil research: The pupil Learning Council researched how children learn, and which learning activities promote pupil engagement, challenge and enjoyment in learning. The research focused on five aspects of learning: fun, challenge, joining in, equipment, and using ICT.

Who was involved: Pupils from the Learning Council in the school.

What the pupil researchers did: The Learning Council devised and distributed a pupil questionnaire on learning. They undertook paired lesson observations using an observation schedule with the senior leadership team, and they undertook some pupil interviews.

Outcomes from the research:

- The Learning Council wrote a formal letter to the head teacher which highlighted the outcomes from their research findings on learning with suggested recommendations, along with other general school improvements.
- For each of the five aspects of learning, they identified useful activities and approaches that would enable pupils to find learning enjoyable, challenging and more engaging.
- The head teacher has subsequently enabled the pupils suggested changes in learning to take place. This has resulted in the recommendations made by the pupils regarding learning being implemented consistently across the entire school.
- Children throughout the school enjoy their learning even more and feel far more empowered as learners.

Cameo of good practice – Enhancing the economic well-being of pupils

School: Tadley Community Primary School, Hampshire

Focus of the pupil research: How to ensure economic well-being topics are areas that pupils throughout the school wanted to learn about.

Who was involved: The members of the pupil Economic Well-Being Team, with pupil representatives from each year group throughout the school. This team also had a governor and parent representative on it. A class teacher, who acted as a facilitator, oversaw the pupil-initiated activities.

What the pupil researchers did: The pupil Economic Well-Being Team devised and distributed a questionnaire to children in the school, which asked them to identify what areas relating to economic well-being they wanted to learn about, and to seek their views on pocket money and saving money.

Outcomes from the research:

- A millionaire's club was formed which entailed a fantasy Stock Exchange for pupils.
- A Dragons' Den/Apprentice competition was run, with each class making a new product to sell and to make a profit, from the £50 funding provided by the PTA.
- A Fantasy Football initiative which involved pupils developing skills in budgeting and pricing to buy and sell players.
- A pupil Journalism Club with a team of pupils producing the 'Writers Block' magazine.
- Information about different careers provided to children in the school.

Cameo of good practice – School Council action research on the school cafeteria

School: Calderstones School, a Specialist Science College, Liverpool

Focus of the pupil research: Improving the school cafeteria and the pupils' dining experience

Who was involved: The members of the School Council

What the pupil researchers did: The School Council devised and distributed a survey to 250 pupils throughout KS3 and KS4, and to 40 sixth-form pupils which asked a series of questions relating to food choice and service; the hygiene and cleanliness of the dining area; and any improvements pupils would like to see being made in the cafeteria. The School Council interpreted and analysed their research findings, and presented the results and outcomes to the head teacher, the senior leadership team and the governing body. The survey results were also publicised on the school's VLE 'Frog' platform for pupils and parents to view the findings.

Outcomes from the research:

The Catering Manager took on board the findings from the School Council research and made the following improvements:

- A healthy salad bar was introduced to the cafeteria.
- Chips were only served once a week and they were oven cooked not fried.
- Meals became healthier and more nutritious.
- Menus were published on the school's VLE 'Frog' platform.
- The quality of food improved, which resulted in meals tasting more like home-cooked meals.

The School Council devised and distributed a pupil survey which focused on pupil satisfaction with the five Every Child Matters outcomes in the school.

The School Council at Calderstones School share their good practice in pupil voice and empowerment with other local school councils, by providing advice and consultancy.

Cameo of good practice – Seeking pupil views on a curriculum subject

School: Alder Community High School, Tameside

Focus of the pupil research: Seeking pupils' views on the English Curriculum in KS4

Who was involved: Year 10 pupils

What the pupil researchers did: Year 10 pupils participated in pupil interviews and undertook a pupil survey. The findings from both methods of research were fed back to the subject curriculum leader for English in the school. The survey focused on seeking pupils' views on the aspects they most enjoyed and those they least enjoyed in the subject; it asked them what they would wish to see improved in English, as well as what they would like to see more of in the subject.

Outcomes from the research:

The subject curriculum leader for English took on board the feedback from the pupils and the following improvements happened:

- More films and moving images are used in English lessons.
- The after-school English coursework club has extended its hours to 2 hours from 1 hour.
- The subject department has enhanced its stock of digital and video cameras.
- The English department has invested in more inspirational English curriculum software for pupil and teacher use in lessons.
- A wider range of up-to-date reading texts have been purchased for pupils.
- English teachers seek more regular pupil feedback at the end of lessons and at the end of a unit of work.
- Extra-curricular opportunities have been further enhanced for pupils, e.g. pupils have worked with a professional actor from The Royal Exchange Theatre in Manchester; pupils participated in an external public speaking competition.

The English department at the school is recognised as a 'lead department' in Tameside in recognition of their hard work and good practice in assessing pupil progress.

Cameo of good practice – exploring activities for young people in the local area

School: Aldridge School – a Science College, Walsall, West Midlands

Focus of the pupil research: How to bring the youth of Aldridge community together to engage in planning and participating in purposeful activities for young people.

Who was involved: Pupils from Aldridge School and from local primary schools in Year 6.

What the pupil researchers did: Pupil views were sought via the School Council and a focused discussion took place between pupils and the local Member of Parliament (MP) to raise his awareness of the need for more activities for young people to engage with, in the local community.

Outcomes from the research:

- Activities are being planned in partnership with the local MP for young people in the local area.
- The Aldridge Youth Parliament has formed a constitution, with clear aims and a rationale.
- The Aldridge Youth Parliament has further strengthened cross-phase partnership working, by engaging Year 6 and Year 9 pupils in joint activities and developments.
- The Aldridge Youth Parliament is proactive and meets regularly as a group of 12 members.
- The Aldridge Youth Parliament was identified by OFSTED as good practice in the school's most recent OFSTED inspection.

Keeping a reflective research journal, diary or log

As a pupil action researcher it is good practice to keep a reflective research journal, or a research diary or a research log. All three perform a similar function, which is to keep an ongoing record of the learning and progress throughout the entire research journey. Table 2.2 provides a useful at-a-glance guide to the different features of each type of research record.

Table 2.2 Keeping a reflective research journal, a research diary or a research log

Type of research record	Reflective Research Journal	Research Diary	Research Log
Definition	This is an ongoing written record of your learning journey and progress as a researcher. It helps to identify your research strengths and any gaps in your research knowledge and skills.	This enables you to keep a powerful detailed account of your research activities from start to finish. It also helps to record any research problems.	This enables you to keep an ongoing record of all the secondary sources of information you have accessed, along with a summary of the main findings from each source.
What to include	• Points of interest from primary and secondary sources of data • Questions you wish to find answers to • Anything new you have learned • Your own personal thoughts (reflection) as a researcher	• Brief description of daily research activities undertaken • List of people who have participated in the research • Secondary sources of data • Findings from the action research (primary sources) you have done • Ideas you wish to follow up • Questions to explore further • Your personal views/opinions • Plan of action • List of research jobs to do	• Key words and search terms • Sources of information • References • Brief summary of main findings from secondary sources of information (data) • Your own thoughts on what you have found out from the secondary sources of data • What you wish to search for or follow up on next
Top tips	• Always carry a small note pad with you that will fit into a pocket to jot down thoughts and data. • Transfer the information from the note pad to either a notebook, or • Develop an electronic reflective research journal using a hand-held personal digital assistant (PDA), or a laptop computer. • Always try to copy up any research notes on the same day, while they are fresh in your mind.	• Highlight in the diary any new knowledge gained from your research. • Record your feelings about and reactions to a significant research experience or activity. • Identify what went well. • Identify what did not go as well. • Suggest how the research activity could be improved. • What you have gained personally from doing the research. • Anything further you want to learn or know about research.	• Always record the date when you searched for secondary sources of information. • Note down where you did the search, e.g. library, internet in school. • Record the search engines used, e.g. Google. • Write out the website address for information found on the internet. • Write out any useful quotes from secondary sources of information, giving page reference, author, title of the article or book.

The majority of pupil action researchers new to the role will find it useful to keep an ongoing reflective research journal. Figure 2.1 provides a model page from a reflective research journal used by secondary school pupils and college students. Figure 2.2 offers a model page from a reflective research journal used by pupils in the primary phase of education. Figure 2.3 provides an example of a page from a research log.

Reflective research journal page
Date of entry:
Reflection activity, event or topic:
Initial thoughts and feelings on today's research:
What I have learned from today's research activity:
What went well today with the research:
Ideas I have for making a change or improvement to the research:
Reflective research question or problem I wish to find the answer to or resolve:
Who can help me with the research question or research problem:
Research term or key word I want to find the definition of:

Figure 2.1 Example of a page from a reflective research journal (secondary)

Reflection on research	Date of entry:

Research activity:

What went well today with the research:

What I have learned from doing the research today:

What I want to find out next in the research:

Figure 2.2 Example of a page from a reflective research journal (primary)

Research log page
Date:
Research topic:
Key words and/or search terms:
Where you found the information: (e.g. library, internet, media)
References:
Brief summary of key points found from secondary sources of information:
Your thoughts about what you have found out from the information search:
What you want to search or follow up on next:

Figure 2.3 Example of a research log page

Some pupil action researchers, as an alternative to a written record, like to keep an electronic record on computer or to maintain a research blog or podcast as an alternative to a handwritten reflective journal.

Sampling

When deciding which research methods to use, it is important to consider how pupil researchers intend to select the sample of participants. Any research sample must be representative of the school's diverse population, e.g. include males and females, different age groups, cultures and ability ranges. Pupil researchers may select their sample randomly or systematically.

Pupils as researchers need to consider whether the size of the chosen sample truly reflects the representative view of the school population of pupils and staff on the topic or issue being researched. For example, interviewing two pupils from each class (the fifth and the tenth pupil on every class register), or surveying all pupils in one key stage, year group or form group.

The bigger the sample or number of participants involved in the research, the more information (data) will have to be analysed and interpreted. The minimum number for a viable sample is 30, and the maximum number is dependent on the size of the organisation and the breadth of the research topic. For example, a sample of between 250 and 300 is likely to be sufficient to distribute a survey or questionnaire to, in a school of 1200 pupils.

Further activities to do with pupils as action researchers relating to Sections 4 and 5 in the relevant pupil research resource pack

1. What types of qualitative and quantitative evidence do the pupil-led research team want to collect?
2. How has the research undertaken by others on the same topic informed what the research pupils wish to do in your own educational setting?
3. On what basis will pupil researchers select their samples of participants in the research?
4. What research methods will the pupil-led action research team utilise in order to undertake this project?
5. Which members of the pupil-led research team will undertake the particular research methods?

Using the action research framework to build a portfolio of evidence

---

The topics covered in this chapter include:

- The key aims in using the action research framework
- Using and completing the action research framework evidence grids
- Top tips for building the action research portfolio of evidence
- The types of evidence to include in the portfolio
- Developing and producing an action plan
- Further activities for pupils as action researchers to think about

---

This chapter is to be used in conjunction with Section 9 of the relevant phase-specific pupil research resource pack, by the teacher overseeing pupil-led action research in the educational setting.

Introduction to the action research framework

The action research framework provided in this chapter focuses on six core themes, essential to the development of pupil researchers, and in enabling change to happen within a school. The six core themes cover:

1. Responsibility
2. Motivation
3. Team work
4. Decision-making
5. Achieving the change
6. Publicising the good practice

Each core theme consists of six good practice descriptors, by which the pupil-led action research team can judge their performance collectively, gathering relevant evidence to confirm each evidence descriptor has been fully met. The action research framework (Table 3.1) is available as a Word document and each theme can be completed at the appropriate stage in the action research process.

Table 3.1 Action research framework

1. RESPONSIBILITY

Good practice descriptors	Examples of evidence to meet each descriptor	Evidence collected for each descriptor	Date
1a. When the action research team agree to investigate a pupil issue it gets done.	Relevant meeting minutes from the action research team or the school council; whole-school pupil consultation or pupil surveys	• •	
1b. Each member of the action research team takes full responsibility for their own actions, working in a 'no blame' culture.	Job description for a pupil action researcher; list of research tasks allocated to pupil action researchers; relevant extracts from pupils' research log or research diary	• •	
1c. The action research team are reliable and are able to keep to the deadlines and timescales set for completing research tasks.	Action plan for the pupil-led action research team project; any interim progress reports on ongoing work of the pupil research team	• •	
1d. All members of the action research team follow the agreed code of conduct relating to confidentiality when gathering evidence from pupils and adults.	The action research team Code of Conduct; written permission from the head teacher to undertake the pupil-led research; signed agreements from each pupil action researcher to follow the Code of Conduct	• •	
1e. The members of the action research team use good judgement to think things through to solve problems during research.	Relevant extracts from the meeting minutes of the pupil-led action research team; extracts from pupils research log or research diary related to problem-solving	• •	
1f. The action research team are respected by pupils, staff and the governors for the work they are doing.	Photographic or video evidence of pupil researchers explaining their role to other pupils in assembly; photographs of any school displays relating to the work of the pupil-led research team; extracts from any pupil researcher job applications	• •	

2. MOTIVATION

Good practice descriptors	Examples of evidence to meet each descriptor	Evidence collected for each descriptor	Date
2a. All members of the action research team experience a great sense of pride in performing their role and they enjoy the added status.	Personal pupil researcher accounts included in their research log or diary; extracts from the mentoring or coaching records for pupil researchers	• •	
2b. Pupil action researchers are appreciated for their contributions to research and receive the necessary praise and recognition from staff, governors and pupils.	Extracts from governing body, senior leadership team or school council meeting minutes; updates on the action research team's work from the school website, newsletters, Live Channel in school, assemblies	• •	
2c. The leader of the action research team inspires the other team members to willingly take on the delegated research tasks with enthusiasm.	Video or audio recording of a pupil action research team meeting; evidence from discussions with the action team leader or member of staff overseeing the work of the team during the on-site visit	• •	
2d. All members of the action research team gain great satisfaction and enjoyment from undertaking the research work.	Relevant personal accounts from pupils' research logs or research diary; evidence gathered from pupil researchers mentoring and coaching sessions; evidence from discussions with pupil researchers, during the on-site visit	• •	
2e. The action research team are provided with good working conditions and sufficient resources to enable them to succeed in seeing the research through to the end.	Evidence of the pupil action research team budget and expenditure throughout the research journey; photographic or video evidence of the team meeting room and work base	• •	
2f. Through undertaking the action research, all team members feel good about themselves, and have grown in self-confidence.	Any feedback from individual pupil researchers' reflective evaluation surveys; relevant extracts from pupils' research logs or research diaries, or from pupils' mentoring and coaching sessions	• •	

Table 3.1 (*Continued*)

3. TEAM WORK

Good practice descriptors	Examples of evidence to meet each descriptor	Evidence collected for each descriptor	Date
3a. All members of the action research team listen to each other's views and opinions, and compromise when there are differing views.	Video or audio recording of a relevant action research team meeting; discussion with or report from the member of staff overseeing the work of the pupil-led action research team	• •	
3b. All members of the action research team willingly share their ideas with other team members.	Relevant extracts from pupil action research team meetings; video or audio recordings from an action research team meeting	• •	
3c. The contributions of all action research team members are valued, however big or small.	Evidence of the pupil researchers' work being recognised through the school's reward system; photographic evidence of any celebration school assemblies	• •	
3d. All members of the action research team cooperate with each other and take turns to do tasks that are sometimes unpopular.	Photographic or video evidence of pupils as action researchers working in pairs or smaller groups to plan or do research activities	• •	
3e. All members of the action research team are clear about their own role, and that of others in the team.	Any reports from the action research team leader or from the staff member overseeing the research work; discussion with pupil researchers during the on-site visit	• •	
3f. Tasks are allocated fairly across the action research team members by the team leader.	Full list of the research tasks allocated to each action research team member; action plan for the research project	• •	

4. DECISION-MAKING

Good practice descriptors	Examples of evidence to meet each descriptor	Evidence collected for each descriptor	Date
4a. All members of the action research team are able to explore a range of options before making a final agreed decision.	Video or audio recording or relevant minutes from an action research team meeting; relevant extracts from pupils' research logs or research diaries; written evidence from the member of staff overseeing the research team's work	• •	
4b. The action research team leader is able to engage team members in purposeful discussion when solving problems.	Video, audio or photographic evidence from a relevant action research team meeting; relevant extracts from the team leader's own research log or research diary	• •	
4c. The action research team can make collective decisions, based on secure and sound evidence, gathered from research.	Photographic evidence, video or audio recording which shows pupils discussing the research data gathered and using this to make decisions; research report extracts	• •	
4d. All members of the action research team recognise and understand the importance of making wise choices in reaching a decision that will benefit other pupils.	Relevant extracts from minutes of pupil research meetings; relevant extracts from pupil researchers' own research logs or research diaries	• •	
4e. The action research team use a good range of approaches to reach an agreed decision, e.g. brainstorm, mind mapping, discussion, reading relevant documents.	Photographic evidence showing different decision-making approaches being used in a pupil research team meeting; example of a mind map or any documentary analysis used to inform decision-making	• •	
4f. Any misunderstandings, mistakes or conflicts of views are dealt with promptly by the team leader in a fair and open manner.	Extracts from minutes of relevant action research team meetings; video clips from a relevant action research team meeting; evidence from teacher or senior manager overseeing the action research team's work which illustrates how any misunderstanding or conflict in the research team has been dealt with by the pupils	• •	

Table 3.1 (*Continued*)

5. ACHIEVING THE CHANGE

Good practice descriptor	Examples of evidence to meet each descriptor	Evidence collected for each descriptor	Date
5a. The action research team make clear to pupils, teachers, governors the reason for doing the research to bring about a change and improvement for other pupils in the school.	Relevant extracts of minutes from any key meetings (governor, senior leadership, staff or school council meetings); extracts from school newsletter, website or Live Channel coverage in school	• •	
5b. The action research team make clear their vision, aims and purpose for achieving the change, to the senior leadership team.	Evidence of presentations to senior leadership team by pupils, e.g. PowerPoint; photographic evidence of pupil researchers presenting to senior leadership meeting	• •	
5c. The action research team develops an action plan, which is shared with the researchers and the senior leadership team.	Action plan for the pupil-led action research team project; extract from school council meeting minutes; relevant extract from the school improvement plan	• •	
5d. The action research team meet formally, once every half term, to review progress towards meeting the research activities on the action plan.	All minutes from the action research team meetings; evidence of ongoing research project progress updates or checks	• •	
5e. The team leader of the action research team presents the key findings and recommendations arising from the research to the senior leadership team and to the governing body/management board.	PowerPoint presentation or other evidence of how the outcomes and findings from the research project have led to change; photographic evidence of team leader delivering findings from research	• •	
5f. The change for the benefit of other pupils in the school happens as a result of the action research team convincing the head teacher that this is the right move.	Any relevant documentary or photographic evidence of the resulting change which has benefited other pupils in the school; feedback from any pupil surveys relating to the benefits of the change	• •	

6. PUBLICISING THE GOOD PRACTICE

Good practice descriptors	Examples of evidence to meet each descriptor	Evidence collected for each descriptor	Date
6a. The action research team meet to discuss and plan their publicity campaign.	Example of meeting notes/minutes that indicate discussion on the publicity campaign; the publicity campaign plan	• •	
6b. The action research team utilises at least **two** different forms of media to publicise the outcomes of their research within the school community.	Blog, podcast or video recording produced by the action research team; power point presentation delivered to different audiences; school newsletter, website or Live Channel features	• •	
6c. The success of the action research team is acknowledged and celebrated by the head teacher and the staff member overseeing the work of the action research team within the school community.	Photographic evidence of head teacher presenting pupil researchers with certificates in assembly for their work; letters sent to pupil action researchers by the member of staff overseeing the teams work, thanking them for their contributions	• •	
6d. The action research team prepare **two** press articles on their research work and outcomes.	Example of the local press article; example of article sent to national press	• •	
6e. The action research team explore and obtain media coverage for their work in the local press, or on local radio or local TV, or with a local Member of Parliament.	Script prepared for a local radio broadcast; evidence of letters sent to local TV station or to the local Member of Parliament by the action research team	• •	
6f. Two members from the action research team deliver a presentation on their research work beyond the school, e.g. to a local cluster group of schools, or at a pupil national, regional or local conference.	Presentation delivered at cluster group meeting or external pupil conference; photographic evidence of members of the action research team sharing their good practice at cluster group meeting or conference	• •	

The key aims in using the action research framework

The two key aims in using the action research framework are as follows:

- to enable pupil researchers, as a team, to keep track of the skills, knowledge and experience gained collectively, throughout the duration of the research project;
- to support the gathering of evidence to build an action research portfolio, for those schools who wish to participate in the national Change for Children Award scheme.

Using and completing the action research framework evidence grids

The leader of the pupil action research team will take overall responsibility for judging whether each evidence descriptor in the six core themes on the action research framework has been fully met. The leader may choose to allocate each of the core themes to members of the action research team, who will gather the relevant evidence to meet each good practice descriptor for their theme. The process will involve pupils as action researchers working cooperatively with other members of the team to collect the necessary evidence.

The teacher or senior member of staff overseeing the work of the pupil-led action research team will offer pupils guidance and advice on the evidence to include, where there is any uncertainty.

Whether the school decides to engage with the national Change for Children Award or not, it is good practice to utilise the action research framework during the lifespan of the pupil-led research project.

Each thematic action research evidence grid provides six descriptors, with examples of the type of evidence to collect, in order to meet the requirements of the good practice evidence descriptors. As the relevant evidence is collected, it should be listed in the third column of the grid. Pupils may wish to include other evidence that has not been exemplified, which is OK to do, providing it is equally relevant.

It is important to put the date when the evidence was collected for each good practice descriptor per theme.

Building an action research portfolio of evidence

The action research portfolio of evidence tells the story of the journey experienced by pupil researchers from start to finish, in order to reach the final goal of making a change or an improvement happen in school for the benefit of other pupils. Building a portfolio of evidence will enable pupils as researchers to share their good practice with pupils in other schools, as well as demonstrating the team's strengths in undertaking action research.

The quality and relevance of the evidence that is included in the portfolio are important. No more than two pieces of evidence are required for each good practice descriptor per core theme. Therefore, if there are six good practice descriptors, then only 12 pieces of evidence in total are required.

Refer to the following top tips to ensure a good-quality action research portfolio of evidence is built.

Top tips for building the action research portfolio of evidence

- A table of contents should be included at the front of the portfolio.
- The portfolio should be divided up into six sections, one for each theme.
- The completed thematic evidence grid should be included at the beginning of each section.
- The collected evidence for each good practice descriptor for the theme should be referenced to correspond with the respective number and letter, e.g. 2b.
- Written and photographic evidence should be placed in punched plastic pockets and be clearly labelled as to which good practice descriptor it relates to.
- Any electronic evidence should be included on a USB flash drive, correctly referenced to the particular theme, e.g. from flash video, blog, podcast.
- Signposting to other relevant electronic evidence that can be found on the school website or Live Channel can be included, but it must be clearly referenced to the relevant good practice evidence descriptor.
- At the end of each section, the completed self-review survey for each core theme should be completed by the pupil researcher or team leader.

Types of evidence to include in the portfolio

The portfolio will only be as good as the quality and reliability of the range of evidence collected to meet each of the six core themes. The forms and types of evidence to gather for the portfolio are as follows:

Written evidence

- Agendas and minutes from meetings
- Progress reports on the work of the action research team
- Action plan
- Code of conduct for ethics of research
- Job description for pupil researcher
- Extracts from pupil's research log, research diary or reflective research journal
- School development plan (relevant sections)
- PowerPoint presentation slides
- Media accounts from the local press
- School newsletters
- Email correspondence between pupil researchers and team leader
- Downloaded information from the school website
- Summary reports on findings from data analysis
- Case studies or cameos of good practice
- External reports and articles on the topic being researched
- Final research report

Multi-media evidence

- Visual evidence on CD, DVD or USB flash drive
- Blogs
- Podcasts
- Flash videos
- Photographic evidence
- Audio recordings
- School Live Channel programmes
- TV programme recording
- Radio broadcast recording

Developing and producing an action plan

The pupil-led action research team needs to develop an action plan which acts as the route map for the work of the team. It will identify the key activities to meet the agreed priorities by all members of the team.

Every time the team meets they need to review the progress towards addressing the priorities and activities on the action plan.

The action plan will clearly identify the distribution of tasks by the team leader across the team. Table 3.2 provides a model framework for an action plan.

Further activities to do with pupils as action researchers relating to Section 9 in the relevant pupil research resource pack

1. What are the benefits of using the action research framework as a pupil-led research team?
2. Which one of the six core themes on the action research framework posed the greatest challenge?
3. What strengths does the pupil-led research team have in relation to the six core themes on the action research framework?
4. What if any changes or additions would you wish to make to the current action research framework?

Table 3.2 Action plan template

Action research core theme	Activity	Responsible pupil researcher	Resources	Timescale (From/To)	Monitoring (Who, When and How)	Success criteria (Impact/outcomes)
1. Responsibility						
2. Motivation						
3. Team work						
4. Decision-making						
5. Achieving the change						
6. Publicising the good practice						

Action Plan framework

Action research activity or task	Link to Change for Children core theme (1 to 6)	Responsible pupil researcher	Resources	Timescale for research project (From/To)	Monitoring (Who, when and how?)	Success criteria (Impact and Outcomes)
Recruit pupil researchers and form a team						
What to research and what is already known on the topic						
Who will do what						
Choosing and trying out the research methods						
Doing the research for real						
Analysing and interpreting the research data						
Presenting the research findings						
Going for the Change for Children Award						

Analysing and presenting the research findings

4

- Analysing and interpreting research findings
- How best to present quantitative and qualitative data
- Explaining and presenting the research findings
- Evaluating the action research experience
- Further activities for pupils as action researchers to think about

This chapter is to be used in conjunction with Sections 6, 7 and 8 of the relevant phase-specific pupil research resource pack, by the teacher overseeing pupil-led action research in the educational setting.

Analysing and interpreting research findings

Analysis refers to the process of describing and translating the evidence gathered from qualitative and quantitative data to make sense of how things are and to find answers to the initial research question. **Interpretation** refers to the process of drawing out important points from the evidence gathered, and to answer the question 'so what?'. There are a number of key factors that need to be taken into account when analysing and interpreting research findings. These are outlined below as top tips.

Top tips on analysing and interpreting research data

- Analyse and interpret data throughout the research project, rather than leaving it all until the end.
- Be clear about what the research has actually found out and what the results show.
- What general observations can be made from the evidence gathered for and against the issue, problem or topic being researched?
- Acknowledge any problems which may have been met when doing the research, and describe briefly how these were overcome.
- Allow enough time to get to grips with the research findings to understand and make better sense of the results.
- Analyse the data gathered **numerically** (number of positive and negative responses to closed questions); by **theme** (where there are similar common points and responses); and by **categories** (the gender, age, key stage of respondents).
- Identify any patterns or common themes emerging from the analysis of research data.
- Only draw conclusions where there is sufficient data to support them.

Analysing and interpreting qualitative data

- Qualitative data, which is likely to be gathered from semi-structured interviews, will need categorising according to the question asked, and sorting and summarising into answers in favour and answers against.
- Use two different coloured highlighter pens, e.g. green for positive 'for' answers, and red for negative 'against' answers, to mark responses on the interviewees schedules, to make information analysis quicker and easier.
- Produce a bullet point list summarising the main findings from the semi-structured interviews, after undertaking the highlighting of text.
- Always indicate the total number of participants interviewed, as well as giving the total responding to each question, and the number 'for' and 'against' in respect of each question response.
- Begin to identify any trends, patterns, similarities or differences from the analysis of the interview data.
- Identify useful and significant quotations from the interviews that will add value to the research results and findings. It may be useful to use phrases such as: 'In the interviews pupils said that . . .', 'When asked the question . . . pupils expressed the view that . . .' and 'The main reasons pupils offered were . . .'.

Analysing and interpreting quantitative data

Quantitative data will be gathered from questionnaires, structured interviews and from any observation schedules collecting numerical data, relating to the frequency of particular activities taking place.

There are three main stages in analysing quantitative information (data).

Stage 1: Data preparation makes the mass of quantitative data collected far more manageable. This may take the form of producing an initial grid which collates the mass of numerical data from respondents per closed question. The grid below provides an example of the layout used for collecting the total evidence from using a research tool such as a questionnaire.

Question number	1	2	3	4	5	6	7	8	9	10	11	12	Question response
All pupils													Yes
													No
Girls													Yes
													No
Boys													Yes
													No

This data from the grid can then be presented in a more user-friendly and interesting format, such as a bar chart or pie chart, in the final written research report or in a PowerPoint presentation.

Stage 2: Data description is where the researcher works from the numerical data in a gird like that shown above, counting the responses in the various categories (questions), calculating proportions or percentages. It is recommended that percentages are used for numbers over 100 in a sample, and numbers are used for expressing data in a sample of less than 100.

Stage 3: Interpreting the data entails giving the totals for each category (question) and pointing out any significant differences or similarities in responses. It also involves drawing out the important points from the analysis of the data in order to answer the key question 'so what?'. Interpretation, based on evidence systematically collected and analysed, aims to move the researcher's thinking forward. Interpretation also entails the researcher comparing their small-scale research findings with secondary sources of information (data) on the same topic.

How best to present quantitative data

A number of choices are available for presenting quantitative data. The most popular methods are tables, graphs, bar charts and pie charts. Familiarity with using an Excel spreadsheet is invaluable for converting data from a table into a range of different formats such as bar charts or pie charts.

When presenting quantitative data it is essential to:

- describe briefly how the data was collected;
- state any problems encountered in collecting the quantitative data and how these were overcome;
- indicate why some data is presented using percentages and other data uses numbers;
- label each table, graph and chart carefully and clearly;
- state what the data is indicating, along with the conclusions that can be drawn.

Figures 4.1, 4.2 and 4.3 illustrate how raw quantitative data can be presented as a graph, bar chart or pie chart. These examples can be shared with pupil researchers when they reach Section 7 in their research resource pack. In addition, you may have other examples from previous research to guide them in this stage of the research journey.

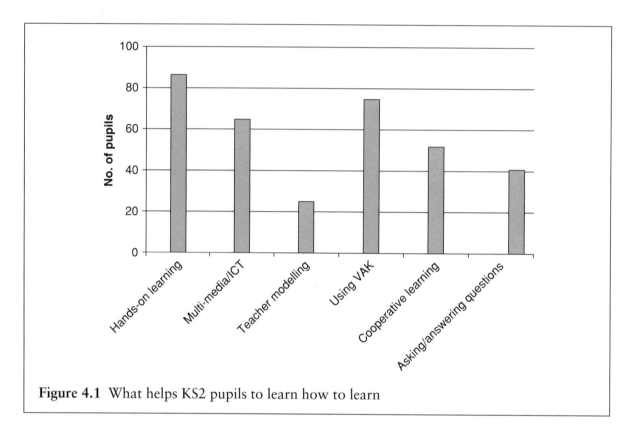

Figure 4.1 What helps KS2 pupils to learn how to learn

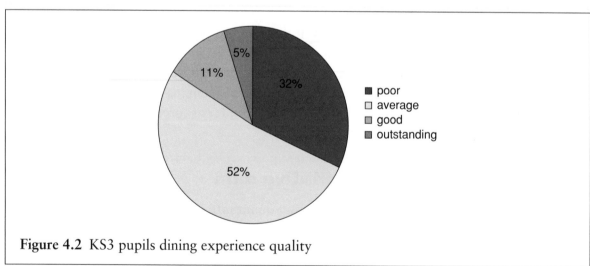

Figure 4.2 KS3 pupils dining experience quality

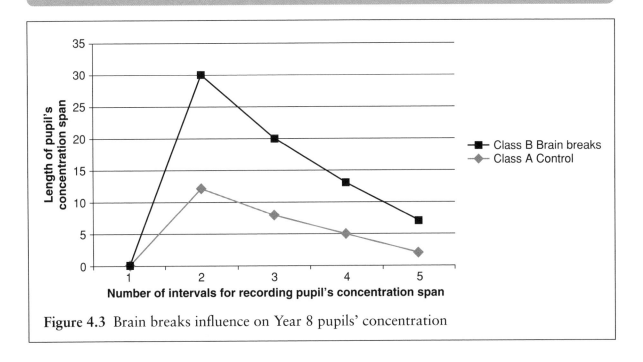

Figure 4.3 Brain breaks influence on Year 8 pupils' concentration

How best to present qualitative data

- Qualitative data needs to be presented clearly, in relation to the research aims or hypothesis.
- It is useful to use headings which relate to question topics or observation topics.
- Under each heading list four or five key findings as bullet points.
- Use short quotations from interviews, but ensure these remain anonymous.

Presenting secondary sources of data

- Always give the source (reference) for any secondary sources of data used.
- Use quotes from secondary sources of information, providing they add something to the research, and always give the exact reference.
- Indicate clearly why the secondary data has been included.
- State what key point the secondary source of information (data) is making.
- Indicate the reliability of the secondary data, e.g. whether it is from official government research findings on the topic, and therefore more reliable than an article in a newspaper, which is based on the writer's opinion.

Explaining and presenting the research findings

Communicating and presenting the results and findings of the research is just as important as doing the actual research. This stage in the research journey should focus on some key questions:

- What has been learned as a result of doing the research on the topic?
- What would others want to know about what has been found out?
- How do pupil researchers know that what they have found out from the research is valid?
- Why do other stakeholders need to know this information?

Pupil researchers will need to explain how the research findings relate to:

- the initial research question or hypothesis;
- the aims of the research;
- other research on the same topic or issue.

Pupils' action research findings aim to provide stakeholders with:

- information that improves their understanding of the factors that influence policy and practice on the topic or issue researched in school;
- ideas that help them make better sense of the current practice in school;
- a set of criteria to evaluate current and future practice in the aspect that has been researched.

When beginning to present and explain the research results and findings to other stakeholders, pupils may wish to open with the statement: 'Here is the evidence which led the pupil research team to reach the following conclusions . . .'.

It is important that the representatives from the pupil-led action research team present the research findings, and not the teacher or other adult who has been overseeing the work of the team.

Prior to presenting and explaining their research findings and results, pupils in the action research team will need to share out the workload. For example, different team members may:

- take responsibility for presenting the findings from the raw data in a more user-friendly format, e.g. pie charts or bar charts;
- plan and prepare the PowerPoint presentation, blog, video or podcast which describes the research journey and the key findings;
- plan and prepare media coverage of the research findings on the school website, Live Channel, school newsletter, or for the local newspaper;
- write a formal letter to the head teacher and the chair of governors, which outlines the results from the research, along with recommendations for change or improvement relating to the issue or topic.

Factors to consider when presenting the results of the team's research

When planning and preparing to present the research results and findings, the pupil action research team will be:

- opening up their research findings to wider scrutiny by a range of different audiences;
- persuading pupils and adults in school to adopt a certain viewpoint;
- clarifying the key points from the research they want to get across to the various stakeholders;
- tailoring the research presentation to suit the different audiences.

What to consider when planning the presentation of the research findings

- Which format of presentation will be used with different audiences, e.g. PowerPoint with video clips, oral presentation from a script, dance drama or a multi-media presentation

- How long the presentation will take to deliver (no longer than 25 minutes)
- Any handouts to be provided to the audience, e.g. PowerPoint slides
- When would be the best time for the presentation to be delivered to the different audiences
- What tables and charts need to be included in the presentation, trying to avoid quantitative data overload
- What information will be fed back to those who participated directly in the research

---

Top tips on planning and delivering a PowerPoint presentation

1. Begin by producing a mind map and ask the pupil research team members to identify what needs to be included in the component parts of the presentation, e.g. introduction (aims and purpose of the research); methods of research used; size of the research sample; key findings; conclusion; recommendations and next steps.
2. Plan and agree upon the PowerPoint structure, e.g. opening (5 minutes); main part (10 minutes) and closing (5 minutes).
3. Decide upon the photographs, cartoons, sound or video clips to be included in the presentation.
4. Do not include too many slides in the presentation; work on the basis of one slide per minute.
5. Use a font size of 20–24 point in slides.
6. Keep the slides simple, with no more than three or four short sentences or bullet points.
7. Avoid using any acronyms or technical jargon in the presentation.
8. Choose a plain background for the slides, which will make the text clear.
9. Practice the presentation before actual delivery to check the time it takes.
10. Ensure the version of PowerPoint is compatible with the computer being used to deliver the presentation.
11. Check the sound level for any video clips or animation before delivery.
12. At the end of delivering the PowerPoint presentation to the audience take just a couple of questions, and ask those with other questions to jot these down and leave them behind for answers to be posted on the educational setting's website at a later date.

Evaluating the pupil-led action research experience

Evaluating and reflecting back on the entire action research experience and project is an important process for all members of the pupil-led action research team to undertake.

Evaluation entails checking whether the aims and objectives of the research have been achieved. It also entails the research team critically examining and judging the effectiveness of the research, its strengths and weaknesses, and how well or otherwise it progressed. Evaluation is concerned with the impact of the overall research activities in terms of enabling a change or improvement to occur, for the benefit of other pupils who raised the issue or concern in the first place.

There are a number of different ways in which action research can be evaluated by pupils overall. Figure 4.4 provides a model evaluation template for pupil use, which relies on a fairly detailed written response. This is likely to be of value to the leader of the pupil-led action research team, and is for completion at the end of the research study or project.

Action research topic:
Start and end dates for the project:
Brief summary of the action research project:
Stakeholders benefiting from the research project outcomes:
Aims and objectives of the action research:
Evidence indicating the success of the action research project:
What aspects of the action research worked well and why?
Any problems that arose from the action research and how they were resolved:
If you did the action research again what would you change or do differently?
Outcomes and impact of the action research project:
How well did the action research process address the six core themes on the action research framework?

Figure 4.4 Evaluating a pupil-led action research project

Other participatory evaluation methods which can be employed by the pupil-led research team may include more practical approaches such as the following:

- **Evaluation wheels** – the leader of the pupil action research team draws a wheel which is divided into a number of sections that relate to key aspects of the research, i.e. each of the six core themes of the action research framework, or each of the stages in the action research cycle. Members of the team as action researchers write in each section of the wheel positive and negative aspects of doing the research project. These are then discussed, and they could also inform the final written report.
- **Evaluation matrices** – each member of the pupil-led action research team scores certain aspects of the research project.
- **Evaluation basket** – the outline of an action researcher is drawn on a large piece of paper. Members of the pupil research team put their responses to a number of key questions in speech bubbles around the drawing of the researcher. The type of questions asked, are as follows:
  - *What have I learned from doing this research?*
  - *What will I take away with me from the research experience?*
  - *What did I like best about the action research experience?*
  - *What I will not wish to repeat again from the research experience?*
- **Evaluation Margolis Wheel** – pupils in the action research team form a circle. In pairs, they discuss the strengths, weaknesses and significant achievements and outcomes of the research work undertaken. They then record their views on sticky notes for sharing more widely, i.e. with future pupil action researchers.

Participatory evaluation, which engages pupils as active and equal research partners, enables them to identify their own success indicators, and to share their research results openly, immediately and in an understandable way.

Further activities to do with pupils as action researchers relating to Sections 6, 7 and 8 in the relevant pupil research resource pack

1. How will the evidence be organised and presented to support meaningful analysis and reflection?
2. How valid and reliable are the interpretation and analysis of the research data gathered, for enabling feasible conclusions to be made?
3. What has the pupil-led action research team got out of doing the research enquiry?
4. Get the pupil-led action research team to produce a top tips list of their own, with a view to helping future pupil action researchers.

A guide to writing the final research report

The topics covered in this chapter include:

- What is a research report?
- The key stages in producing a research report
- Top tips on what to include in a research report
- Checklist of reflective questions to review the research
- Other formats for reporting research findings
- Further activities for pupils as action researchers to think about

This chapter is to be used in conjunction with Section 7 of the relevant phase-specific pupil research resource pack, by the teacher overseeing pupil-led action research in the educational setting.

What is a research report?

A research report tells the story of the research journey in exploring, investigating and finding out the answers to a research question or problem. The author of the final research report must not assume that the reader of the report already knows something about the topic. Therefore, the report must be written in a clear, concise, jargon-free and understandable format.

Research report checklist to use with the pupil action research team

- Confirm who the research report will be read by.
- Help bring together all the information (data) gathered from the research.
- Guide the pupil researchers in writing up this information (data).
- Give guidance on who is best to write the overall final research report.
- Help allocate report sections to members of the research team to write up.
- Support pupils in determining what the length of the final research report will be.
- Agree with pupils the format in which the research report will be produced.
- Advise pupils to summarise the key points arising from the research.
- Help pupils agree upon what quantitative data will be included in the report.
- Guide pupils in how best to present qualitative information in the report.

- Allow pupils to produce the first draft of the research report.
- Proof-read the first draft of the research report for the pupils.
- Guide pupils in redrafting the research report and the front cover design.
- Print the required number of copies of a summary version of the research report, as well as copies of the full report.
- Help to distribute the report to the various interest groups, e.g. school council, head teacher, chair of governors, parent council, key staff.

Top tips on what to include in a research report

Section of the research report	What to include/key questions
Title of the research report	The report title should convey the theme of the research and the nature of the study clearly.
Introduction	Background and context to the issue or problem being researched. Why is the topic of interest? Reasons why the research was undertaken. What was significant about the topic of study? The research goals (aim, objectives, purpose). Produce initial research question(s) to be explored.
Literature review	What is already known about the topic or issue from previous research (in school or beyond)? What can be learned from any previous research, and what does it add?
Hypothesis	What do you expect to find out, e.g. the claim to knowledge and the answers you seek to the problem or issue of concern?
Research methods	The research methods chosen, with reasons for choice and their appropriateness to the topic or issue. How reliable the research methods used were. How you went about doing the research. How you decided on the sample of participants engaging in the research. The timescale for the research work. The ethics shown in doing the research with pupils and staff in school.

Results and findings	What you found out from doing the research.
	Present the results and findings in an interesting way, e.g. use charts, graphs, tables. Present qualitative descriptive findings in an organised way, e.g. using bullet point lists to summarise key findings.
Discussion	What do the results and findings mean? Are they reliable?
	Answering the research question(s) posed.
	Whether there is anything important arising from the results and findings, or if there are any surprises. Is the hypothesis proved/disproved?
	How your findings and results compare with any previous research done on the same topic.
	Analysis and interpretation of the findings from the evidence gathered (not descriptive).
Conclusions	What is the significance of the research?
	Has the problem or issue been resolved?
	How useful has the research been?
	Have you achieved what you set out to do?
	What have you discovered, and what have you learned from this research? So what?
Recommendations	What key recommendations are you making?
	Are the recommendations feasible and doable?
	What further research, if any, might be useful?
	Next steps?
References	Full list of books and documents you have used during the research project.
Appendices	Include tables, 'raw data', blank questionnaire, blank interview and observation schedules, photographs, and any other material that does not fit in with the main body of the research report.

Table 5.1 provides a blank research report framework for pupils to utilise.

Table 5.1 Research report framework

Report author:	School or college:
Report title:	
Introduction (200 words)	
Literature review	
Hypothesis	
Research methods (500 words)	
Results and findings	
Discussion (500 words)	
Conclusion (200 words)	
Recommendations	
References	
Appendices	

Checklist of reflective questions to review the research

The following list of questions can be used as prompts by the team leader and all members of the pupil-led action research team, to review whether all the required information has been collected and included in the final research report:

- Did I/we collect the necessary information (data) as planned?
- What problems did I/we have in gathering the information (data)?
- Could I/we have used other research methods?
- Did I/we gather information (data) from the right people, or were there others from whom I/we should have gathered views and opinions?
- Have I/we interpreted and presented the information in the best way?
- Am I/are we able to discuss the information gathered freely with others?
- Have I/we used too much jargon or technical words in the report?
- Does the research report need tailoring to suit different audiences?
- If I/we did this research again, would I/we do anything differently?
- What have I/we gained from doing the research project?

Other formats for reporting research findings

Although a written final research report is an essential requirement for those schools and other educational settings wishing to engage with the national Change for Children Award, other ways of delivering the findings from the research are permissible:

- Video presentation
- Blog
- Podcast
- Text messaging
- Dance or drama production, including a musical
- Puppet show (for younger children)
- Poetry
- Art display
- Exhibition, including photographs
- Posters and postcards
- Storytelling/storyboard
- Diary accounts
- Electronically via the school website or Live Channel plasma screen
- School newsletters
- Verbal report
- Multi-media – a mixture of some of the above methods

Further activities to do with pupils as action researchers relating to Section 7 in the relevant pupil research resource pack

1. How will the pupil-led action research team ensure that they reflect on the outcomes and implications of the research before writing the report?
2. How will the pupil-led research team decide upon what to include and exclude from the final research report?
3. How can the teacher overseeing the work of the pupil-led action research team best support the production of the final research report?
4. What will be the best method of sharing the research results with the majority of pupils in the school?

6

Change happens: rewarding good practice

This chapter is to be used in conjunction with Section 9 of the relevant phase-specific pupil research resource pack, by the teacher overseeing pupil-led action research in the educational setting.

Understanding the process of change

Change, as an ongoing process, aims to improve practice, provision and/or introduce new school policies. Change challenges existing beliefs, values and practice, and therefore results in some pupils and teachers feeling unsure about the future change.

A pupil-led action research team will have had a huge impact in influencing and enabling the change to happen, for the benefit of other pupils in the school, through the research work undertaken. Pupil researchers will have made several worthwhile contributions to the various stages in the change process in the school. Figure 6.1 illustrates the stages in the change process that schools go through, in making changes and improvements for pupils and staff.

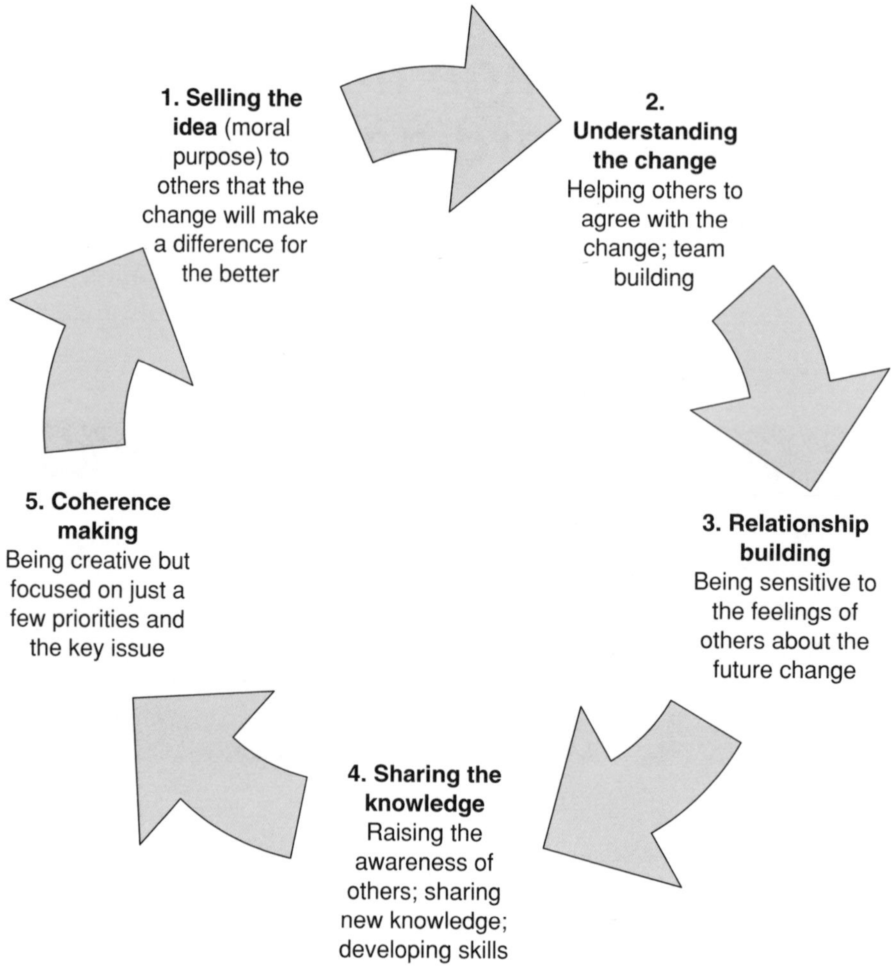

1. Selling the idea (moral purpose) to others that the change will make a difference for the better

2. Understanding the change
Helping others to agree with the change; team building

3. Relationship building
Being sensitive to the feelings of others about the future change

4. Sharing the knowledge
Raising the awareness of others; sharing new knowledge; developing skills

5. Coherence making
Being creative but focused on just a few priorities and the key issue

Figure 6.1 Stages in the change process

Evaluating and reviewing the action research process

Evaluation refers to judging the effectiveness, strengths and weaknesses of engaging in and undertaking the action research project. It also helps to indicate how well the action research is progressing, and the impact and outcomes the research has on influencing school decision-making and bringing about change. Figure 6.2 provides a self-review survey for each member of the pupil action research team to complete, in order to evaluate their experience in participating in the research project. This completed survey needs to be included in the action research portfolio of evidence, where a school decides to engage in the national Change for Children Award.

Are you: male ☐   female ☐   Year Group ☐   Form/class ☐

Please answer the following questions
The survey is to be included in the action research portfolio of evidence

QUESTIONS

1. What new skills have you learned by working in an action research team?

2. What has been the most enjoyable aspect of engaging in the action research process?

3. Was there any aspect of the action research project that you found more difficult to manage?

4. How helpful was the action research framework to use?

5. How useful was it having a teacher to oversee the research project?

6. How valuable was the initial session on research methods?

7. What other information and guidance would you wish to see included in the pupil research resource pack?

8. Would you feel able to coach or mentor another pupil doing research?

9. Is there anything else you wish to comment on in relation to pupil-led action research?

Thank you for completing this survey.

Figure 6.2 Pupil researcher self-review survey

Meeting the requirements of the national Change for Children Award

Those schools that have decided to work towards achieving the national Change for Children Award will have already registered to participate in the scheme, in addition to making an initial part-payment (half the total cost of the award). The award is only available from Educational Consultancy & Management (ECM) Solutions, who externally assess and validate the school's good practice in pupil-led action research.

In order to meet the requirements of the award scheme, various stages need to have been completed. Figure 6.3 illustrates the milestones that the pupil-led action research team will have had to progress through in order to be eligible for achieving the award.

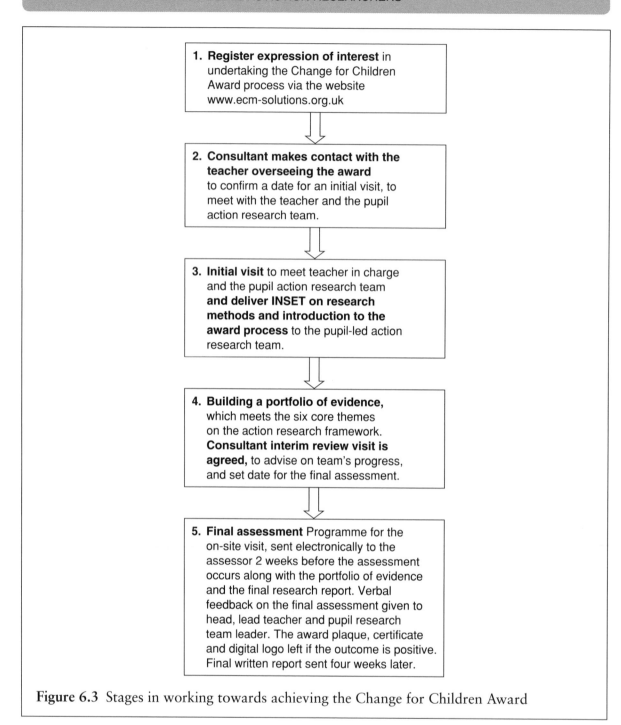

Figure 6.3 Stages in working towards achieving the Change for Children Award

Preparing for the off-site external assessment

The leader of the pupil action research team, in partnership with the teacher who is overseeing the work of the team, will need to ensure the following evidence is sent to the external assessor electronically, at least two weeks before the final on-site assessment takes place:

- the final written research report;
- the pupil research team's action plan;
- all the agendas and minutes from the pupil action research team meetings;
- the electronic portfolio of evidence with the six completed action research framework evidence grids;

- a zip folder, CD, DVD or USB flash drive containing all the necessary multi-media and documentary evidence to meet the evidence descriptors on the six core thematic grids;
- the action research team's completed pupil researcher self-review surveys;
- signposting to relevant information on the educational setting's website.

The external assessor will provide a postal address and a secure email address to the teacher in charge, to enable the evidence to be sent to him or her on time. The external assessor will acknowledge safe receipt of the evidence by email. The electronic documentary and multi-media evidence will be referred to and reflected in the external assessor's final written report.

Preparing for the on-site external assessment

The external assessor must receive the planned programme for the final on-site assessment electronically at least two weeks before the date of the visit.

The pupil action research team, in partnership with the teacher overseeing the award process, will need to negotiate, agree and organise whom and what the external assessor will see during the on-site final assessment day.

The aim and purpose of the on-site external assessment

The aim of the on-site assessment is to enable the pupil action research team to highlight their good practice. Its purpose is to enable the external assessor to:

- gather the views and opinions of a range of different stakeholders, on the benefits of the resulting change or improvement, as a result of the work of the pupil-led action research team;
- observe first-hand the outcomes and impact of the change or the improvement;
- gain an overall impression of how the culture and ethos of the school promotes pupil voice and participation, through pupil-led action research to inform school decision-making;
- check out whether the electronic evidence in the action research portfolio is reflected in the school's everyday policy and practice, in relation to empowering pupils as active participants in the running and work of the educational setting;
- reach an overall view about whether the school has fully met all the requirements in order to achieve the national Change for Children Award, which is valid for three years.

The following example, provides a model of a programme for the final on-site external assessment.

Example of a programme for the on-site final external assessment

8.30 Arrival of the external assessor at the school. Welcome and introductions

8.45 Discussion with the head teacher, a governor and the teacher overseeing the work of the pupil action research team

9.15 A tour of the school escorted by two members of the pupil action research team, or from the school council

10.00 Discussion with the pupil action research team about their work

10.30 Break and time for reflection for the external assessor

11.00 Discussion with a group of pupils from across the school who have benefited from the change or improvement

11.30 Discussion with key staff/members of the school workforce who have knowledge of and first-hand experience of the work of the pupil action research team

12.00 Lunch

13.00 Discussion with a group of parents about pupil 'voice' and pupils' participation in school decision-making

13.30 Snapshot observation of either a meeting of the pupil action research team meeting or of a school council meeting

14.00 Reflection time for the external assessor

14.30 Brief verbal feedback to the head teacher on the assessment findings. Departure of the external assessor

Following the on-site assessment, the external assessor will add this evidence to the final award report. The assessor will send the draft award report via email to the teacher overseeing the pupil action research team for checking for accuracy, four weeks after carrying out the final on-site assessment.

Once the final award report is confirmed as being accurate by the leader of the pupil action research team, the digital award logo will be sent to the school. A date and time will be agreed for the external assessor to revisit the school to present the Change for Children Award plaque and certificate.

Further activities to do with pupils as action researchers relating to Section 9 in the relevant pupil research resource pack

1. How far did the pupil action research team face any barriers or obstacles to making the change happen, and if so, how were these overcome?

2. What has been the impact in the school of the work of the pupil-led action research team?

3. How far do you think the findings and results from the pupil action research team influenced the head teacher in enabling the change or improvement to happen?

4. What else could the head teacher do to enable pupils to do more action research projects in the school in the future?

5. Overall, what went well with the action research project?

6. What issue or aspect of the school's work would pupils as researchers wish to explore next?

Glossary

Action research is a method of enquiry or investigation to increase understanding of an issue to bring about a change or improvement for the benefit of others.

Analysis is the process of examining information (data) to establish what it means, to make sense of it, and to find answers to the initial research question.

Bias refers to the personal views of the researcher influencing the questions they ask participants.

Blog refers to a short video production which aims to get key messages across to a wide audience.

Closed question is one that limits the responses that can be made, e.g. yes or no answers.

Coding is a system used to make qualitative data far more manageable to process and analyse.

Content analysis is the process employed by researchers when they are using secondary sources of data to check how far written information or an advertisement misleads the reader or distorts the truth.

Data is any form of information, numerical (quantitative) or descriptive (qualitative), which is used by researchers to make decisions.

Dependent variable is any factor that shows the effect of an influence.

Delegation is the process of entrusting someone else with the appropriate responsibility for doing a particular activity or task.

Direct observation is where the researcher observes action without joining in with the action themselves.

Ethics in research refers to making sure that the interests, views and identity of those agreeing to participate in research are protected and remain confidential. It also relates to ensuring no harm or distress is caused as a result of pupils or adults taking part in the research.

Experiment is a research approach which aims to discover the effect of variables on participants' behaviour, for example.

Fact is a proven belief based on information (data) which has been collected and analysed.

Hypothesis is a possible answer or an explanation to a research question. It enables a researcher to check out the truth. A hypothesis is optional and is dependent on the topic or issue being explored.

Independent variable is a factor which exerts an influence on someone or on a situation.

Interpretation refers to drawing out important points from the research evidence gathered. It helps to answer the researcher's question 'so what?'.

Myth is an unproven belief based on an idea or prejudice.

Observation is a research method that involves looking and listening very carefully to action, e.g. what is taking place in a lesson.

Open question is one which does not limit the response from a participant.

Participant observation is undertaken by a researcher who is also part of the action which is being observed by them.

Podcast refers to an audio or video recording in a series of episodes, which describes the steps and stages taken in relation to producing a final product, or undertaking a particular task or activity, such as an action research project.

Primary sources of data are evidence which is collected directly by a researcher who undertakes an interview, observation, a research experiment, or issues a questionnaire or survey.

Qualitative data is non-numerical descriptive information gathered from research.

Quantitative data is quantifiable numerical information gathered from research.

Questionnaire is a list of closed questions, which are usually given in written form.

Reflection is the process of looking back on a research experience, for example, in order to think about what we have learned. It is the bridge between thinking and actions.

Research is the process of collecting and analysing information to increase understanding of the topic or issue under study. It also includes addressing an issue of concern, asking and answering questions or solving a problem.

Sampling is the process of selecting a suitable subset of the population in order to gain information about the wider view of the whole population.

Secondary sources of data are information that has been collected by others, e.g. newspaper articles, official government reports, national statistics.

Semi-structured interview uses a core of key open questions with the option of the researcher being able to follow up on responses by probing further.

Theory is a belief that has not yet been proved.

Triangulation is the process which uses a number of different research approaches in order to cross-check data in order to increase the validity of the research information.

Variable is any factor that can make a difference to situation or participants, e.g. being male, female, of a particular age or ability.

References and further reading

Cheminais, R. (2008) *Engaging Pupil Voice to Ensure that Every Child Matters: A Practical Guide*. Abingdon: Routledge.

Dallope, F. and Gilbert, C. (1993) *Children's Participation in Action Research*. London: ENDA.

Drever, E. (1995) *Using Semi-Structured Interviews in Small-Scale Research: A Teacher's Guide*. Edinburgh: Scottish Council for Research in Education.

Economic and Social Research Council (2003a) *What Makes a Good Lesson and a Good Teacher?* Communicating – Consulting Pupils Project Newsletter No. 8, pp. 2–3. Cambridge: ESRC.

Economic and Social Research Council (2003b) *Consulting through Questionnaires*. Communicating – Consulting Pupils Project Newsletter No. 9, pp. 1–3. Cambridge: ESRC.

Fielding, M. and Bragg, S. (2003) *Students as Researchers: Making a Difference*. Cambridge: Pearson Publishing.

Frost, R. and Handscomb, G. (2009) Active enquiring minds: Empowering young researchers. Paper presented to the International Congress for School Effectiveness and Improvement (ICSEI), Vancouver, 4–7 January.

Handscomb, G. (2009) *Active Enquiring Minds: Guidance for Adults Seeking to Develop and Support Young Researchers in Schools*. Chelmsford: Essex County Council.

Hopkins, D. (2008) *A Teacher's Guide to Classroom Research*, 4th edition. Maidenhead: Open University Press.

Kellett, M. (2005a) *How to Develop Children as Researchers. A Step-by-Step Guide to Teaching the Research Process*. London: Paul Chapman Publishing.

Kellet, M. (2005b) *Children as Active Researchers: A New Research Paradigm for the 21st Century?* Cambridge: Economic and Social Research Council.

Kirby, P. (1999) *Involving Young Researchers: How to Enable Young People to Design and Conduct Research*. York: York Publishing Services.

Kirby, P. (2004) *A Guide to Actively Involving Young People in Research: For Researchers, Research Commissioners and Managers*. Eastleigh: Involve/PK Research Consultancy.

Langley, P. (1988) *Doing Social Research: A Guide to Coursework*. Ormskirk: Causeway Press.

Morgan, J., Williamson, B., Lee, T. and Facer, K. (2007) *Enquiring Minds*. Bristol: Futurelab.

Mugo, F.W. *Sampling in Research*. http://www.socialresearchmethods.net/tutorial/Mugo/tutorial.htm (accessed 20 December 2010).

Munn, P. and Drever, E. (1996) *Using Questionnaires in Small-Scale Research: A Teacher's Guide*. Edinburgh: Scottish Council for Research in Education.

Payton, S. and Williamson, B. (2008) *Enquiring Minds: Professional Development Materials*. Bristol: Futurelab.

Ruddock, J. (2003) *Pupil Voice is Here to Stay!* London: Qualifications and Curriculum Authority.

Simpson, M. and Tuson, J. (1995) *Using Observations in Small-Scale Research. A Beginner's Guide*. Edinburgh: Scottish Council for Research in Education.

Wilkinson, J. (2000) *Children and Participation: Research, Monitoring and Evaluation with Children and Young People*. London: Save the Children.

Worrall, S. (2000) *Young People as Researchers: A Learning Resource Pack*. London: Save the Children.